AMERICAN POETS PROJECT

AMERICAN POETS PROJECT

IS PUBLISHED WITH A GIFT IN MEMORY OF

James Merrill

AND SUPPORT FROM ITS FOUNDING PATRONS

Sidney J. Weinberg, Jr. Foundation

The Berkley Foundation

Richard B. Fisher and Jeanne Donovan Fisher

A. R. Ammons

selected poems

david lehman editor

AMERICAN POETS PROJECT

THE LIBRARY OF AMERICA

Poems copyright © 1965, 1972, 1974, 1975, 1977, 1981, 1982, 1983, 1987, 1990, 1993, 1996, 1997 by A. R. Ammons. Copyright © 2005, 2006 by John R. Ammons. See page 125 for permission acknowledgments.

The paper used in this publication meets the minimum requirements of the American National Standard for Information Sciences—Permanence of Paper for Printed Library Materials, ANSI Z39.48—1984.

Design by Chip Kidd and Mark Melnick.
Frontispiece: Photo by Thomas Victor

Library of Congress Cataloging-in-Publication Data:
    Ammons, R. R., 1926–2001.
    [Poems, Selecitons]
        Selected Poems / A. R. Ammons ; David Lehman, edior.
    p. cm—(American poets project ; 20)
    ISBN 1-931082-93-6 (alk. paper)
        I. Lehman, David, 1948– II. Title. III. Series.
PS3501.M6 A6   2006
811'.54—dc22
2006040807

10 9 8 7 6 5 4 3 2 1

A. R.
Ammons

CONTENTS

INTRODUCTION

A. R. Ammons had reason to consider himself, as he capriciously put it in a late poem, a "drab pot"—"top bard" spelled backwards partly to conceal and partly to revel in the distinction. A solitary figure, self-made and largely self-taught, he approached the centers of literary industry as an outsider and from a distance. Without ever quite overcoming his distrust of the establishment, he accepted the recognition that came his way—the Bollingen Prize, a MacArthur Fellowship, the National Book Award (twice) —though the accolades did little to lessen the state of pent-up anxiety that Ammons identified as an impetus for his writing, if not itself a source of inspiration. By the time of his death in February 2001, a week after his 75th birthday, Ammons had long held a titled professorship at Cornell, where he was well-loved. His poems were and continue to be championed by formidable critics (Harold Bloom, Helen Vendler) and a diverse array of poets. (Douglas Crase: "What I learned from Archie was that I didn't have to write poems about Italy.") Yet possibly because he stands outside of schools and affiliations and resists classification by region or genre, Ammons's poetry remains for many readers a discovery they make on their own and love all the better for it.

The best of Ammons's poems can have a transforming effect—they make you want to take a walk along a bay and chronicle your impressions, or compose a hymn in his manner or a meditation on a word like *sanctuary* or *longing*, or start a diary in skinny lines as Ammons does in *Tape for the Turn of the Year* (1965), which he typed on a roll of adding-machine tape, the width of the tape serving as the arbitrary but fixed restraint determining the shape of the poem. Ammons, who loves walking in his poems as greatly as in their differing ways Wordsworth and Frost do, developed a distinctive style in keeping with his peripatetic habits. "The perfect journey is / no need to go," he will say cheerily before taking a walk "between the pine / colonnades / up the road on the hill" where the breeze can be counted on to sift "figurations from the snow." The Ammons manner is casual, direct, at ease in nature; his diction unpretentious and capable of abrupt shifts. He is often witty, sometimes bawdy, with a wide range of reference, on a perpetual quest to find forms capacious enough for an imagination intent on finding a place for everything. He values, above all things, motion and momentum in his innovative prosody. A short poem may pivot on a reversal (sparked by "so" or "nevertheless") and end on an epiphany. A long poem is likelier to feature more authorial self-consciousness ("today / I feel a bit different: / my prolog sounds phony & / posed"), more down time for jokes, recipes, weather reports, assorted asides ("anybody doesn't believe in / reality should / try to start a dead car / on a 10-degree / morning"), and an even more intimate relation to the reader. "Ideally," he writes near the end of *Tape for the Turn of the Year*, from which I have been quoting, "I'd / be like a short poem: / that's a fine way / to be: a poem at a / time: but all day / life itself is bending, / weaving, changing, / adapting, failing, / succeeding."

Born in Whiteville, North Carolina, in 1926, the youngest of a tobacco farmer's three surviving children, Archie Randolph Ammons grew up on the family farm during the meanest years of the Great Depression. He had two sisters; two brothers died as infants, one of them when Archie was four years old. The traumatic memory of his younger brother's death enters Ammons's poetry in "Easter Morning" (1981) and again in *Glare* (1997), in the passage that gives the book its title, where the poet recollects the desperate folk ritual to which his parents resorted: they split a sapling and passed the ailing child through the split tree-trunk. But the boy didn't recover. "One Must Recall as One Mourns the Dead" (from *The Snow Poems*, 1977) achieves sublime pathos by refusing to mourn:

> do not mourn the dead too much who bear no
> knowledge, have no need or fear of pain,
>
> and who never again must see death
> come upon what does not wish to die

The elegiac strain in Ammons's poetry is surpassed only by the countermining impulse to say yes to the universe. "I know / there is / perfection in the being / of my being, / that I am / holy in amness / as stars or / paperclips," he writes in "Come Prima." The knowledge coexists with the recognition that the universe moves "from void to void" and that void and being are indistinguishable. Yet the poet's elation survives. Determined to convert fear into praise, and anxiety into poetry, Ammons balances his scientist's skepticism with the Romantic conception of the imagination as

redemptive of, or compensatory for, the bitterness of actu-
ality. Like Robert Frost, he knows nature too intimately to
sentimentalize it or flinch in the face of its cruelties. But he
is less chilly than Frost. The transcendent "radiance" he
considers in "The City Limits" illuminates equally a sub-
lime landscape or "the glow-blue // bodies and gold-
skeined wings of flies swarming the dumped / guts of a nat-
ural slaughter or the coil of shit . . ." Despite the ugliness
that it encounters, the "radiance" never "winces from its
storms of generosity."

The young Archie—everyone who knew him called
him Archie, and it is hard to think of him any other way—
heard hellfire sermons in church each Sunday. In *Glare* he
makes light of them:

> sixty years ago, I used to hear every
> Sunday that Jesus was coming: the
>
> preacher wasn't specific but said it
> could be any hour or minute but
>
> certainly before next Sunday: next
> Sunday would come but no Jesus, and
>
> the preacher never seemed embarrassed
> for his disaster quotient was as high
>
> as ever . . .

Ammons's equanimity here is a triumph of tone. The re-
peated prophecy that "Jesus was coming" terrified the
young man. The hymns he heard as a boy at the Spring
Branch Fire-Baptized Pentecostal Church had an influence
on his poetry, even if it was mostly unconscious.

Around the time of President Roosevelt's death in
April 1945, while serving aboard a destroyer escort in the
South Pacific, the 19-year-old sailor had an experience of

almost religious intensity. Sitting on the bow of the ship anchored in a bay, he found himself staring at the land, the water level and the life beneath it, and "the line inscribed across the variable land mass, determining where people would or would not live, where palm trees would or could not grow." It suddenly struck him that "the water level was not what it was because of a single command by a higher power, but because of an average result of a host of actions—run-off, wind currents, melting glaciers." In that moment Ammons felt all the mystery and faith and passion of religion attached to a scientific explanation of the universe. He wrote his first serious poems as a result of this "interior illumination."

In many subsequent works Ammons fuses a religious impulse with scientific knowledge, substituting facts for articles of faith, arriving at sublime ends through secular means, in a triumph of wonderment. (See, for example, "Cascadilla Falls.") He writes about matters of scientific and philosophical complexity as few American poets have done, yet never without the homespun humor and sly wit that sometimes raise bantering wordplay to transcendent paradox: He may "see no / god in the holly, hear no song from the / snowbroken weeds," as he admits in "Gravelly Run." Nevertheless, "somehow it seems sufficient." Ammons's brand of the American religion can be summed up in the title of a late poem: "God Is the Sense the World Makes without God."

After his discharge from the Navy, Ammons attended Wake Forest on the GI Bill and majored in science. In 1949 he married his Spanish teacher, Phyllis Plumbo. He made his living at a variety of occupations, none of them remotely literary. He worked briefly as the principal of the tiny elementary school in Cape Hatteras and later managed his father-in-law's biological glass factory in southern

New Jersey. At the University of California at Berkeley, where he and Phyllis spent three semesters in the early 1950s, he benefited from the warm support of Josephine Miles, a greatly underrated poet and teacher, with whom he corresponded faithfully for years thereafter. (Miles, who suffered from rheumatoid arthritis so severe that it confined her to a wheelchair, is the spirit presiding over Ammons's early poem "A Crippled Angel.") In 1955 Ammons published *Ommateum*, his first book of poems, with Dorrance, a vanity press. A total of 16 copies were sold in the next five years. Not until 1963, when he was 37, did Ammons's vocation and avocation dovetail. *Expressions of Sea Level*, his second collection, came out that year from Ohio State University Press, and Archie was invited to give a reading at Cornell. The faculty liked what they heard and Archie accepted a low-level teaching appointment to begin the next fall. Critical recognition followed; Ammons rapidly went from nearly total obscurity to wide acclaim.

Though his intellectual curiosity was boundless, Ammons remained academically incorrect in some fundamental and attractive way. He groused about "the whole business of getting degrees in the writing of poetry," likening the practice to "putting chains on butterflies' wings." In retrospect the years of obscurity looked pretty good. "In business I knew I was a fish out of water and I had many a miserable day," he once told me. "But I felt more like a writer then. In universities I always felt the presence of a cottony wad of verbalisms between the poet and the poem—the constant presence of all kinds of extraneous and farfetched theories and explanations of poems. Everything is discursive opinion instead of direct experience. There's something to be said in favor of working in isolation in the real world." The self that sustains itself on speech reigns as supreme in Ammons's universe as in Emerson's or Stevens's, and feels itself to be as isolated.

In poem after poem Ammons obsesses over the philosophical question of "the one and the many" as others may obsess over their favorite basketball team or popular singer. Consider the opening of "The Fairly High Assimilation Rag" (1983): "Plato derives the many from the one and Aristotle / the one from the many." In a nutshell, the question of the one and the many is whether reality inheres in countless particulars (the many) or whether there is a motion and a spirit (the one) rolling through all things. Understood as a tug-of-war between unity and diversity, the question has an immediate application to the American scene. "They ask why I'm so big on the // one:many problem, they never saw one: my readers: what do they / expect from a man born and raised in a country whose motto is *E / pluribus unum*?" In a bravura section of *Sphere*, Ammons translates "the one and the many" into figures (a mountain or "an isosceles triangle," with the peak standing for unity and the base for diversity) and ratios (with "base:periphery: diversity" on one side and "peak:center:symbol:abstraction" on the other). To Ammons, this is a way not only to renew ceaselessly a fundamental question about the nature of reality but to organize the world into poems. Many of his come down squarely on the "many" side of the ledger. Not "a whit manic" about Whitman's influence, Ammons uses the inventory for the same reason it appealed to the author of "Song of Myself": it is democratic, anti-hierarchical, a gathering of particulars, a reveling in what is at the "base" of the triangle, "base" understood as having an ethical or class meaning as well as a geometrical one. "Shit List" (1982) is an apt illustration of the irreverent Ammons inventory. On the other hand, when the poet reaches the "summit," as he does in the poem on the dedication page of *Sphere* ("For Harold Bloom") he feels a certain desolation or emptiness:

> for the word *tree* I have been shown a tree
> and for the word *rock* I have been shown a rock,
> for stream, for cloud, for star
> this place has provided firm implication and
>   answering
>   but where here is the image for *longing*:

Staring into space and into the sun from the "high nakedness," the poet is forced to acknowledge that "nothing answered my word *longing*." The word *nothing* recurs in this poem, its meaning as complex as a primal word signifying itself and its opposite. Ammons's late friend Jerald Bullis paraphrased Ammons's *nothing* as "the plenum of factual reality: the universe cleansed of supernatural agency."

Harold Bloom minimizes the influence of William Carlos Williams on Ammons, but it is there not only in allusion (on the first page of *Garbage*, for example) but in the pacing of his poems and in his conception of the poet. These lines from Williams's "The Wind Increases" anticipate a favorite Ammons trope:

> Good Christ what is
> a poet—if any
>   exists?
> a man
> whose words will
>   bite
>   their way
> home—being actual
>
> having the form
>   of motion

For the subtitle of *Sphere: The Form of a Motion* (1974), Ammons liked crediting a Cornell faculty meeting ("Can someone put that in the form of a motion?"), but these lines may have lurked in the back of his mind.

Ammons dispenses with rhyme and meter, disdains the "sonnet or some fucking cookie-cutter" form, and rejects the notion that American literature is part of a larger entity encompassing the English literary tradition. An entertaining digression in *Glare* begins with the remark that "I / cannot, to pause momentarily, bear the Brits," as if he might provide the counter-note to Philip Larkin's grouchy view of America. The contempt might have been mutual: Larkin wrote in strict form, and the principle of restraint applies even to his output, which was modest though choice; the prolific Ammons is wholly committed to free verse, contriving ways to enact motion, process, and flow as guiding principles. Ammons capitalizes on the humble colon, using it as an all-purpose punctuation mark with the effect of a continual postponement of closure. In poems of the great middle period—"The City Limits," "Triphammer Bridge," and *Sphere*, to name three—he writes in three-line stanzas that resemble a species of *terza libre*: a rhymeless version of the stanza unit of Shelley's "Ode to the Western Wind." Like Robert Creeley, a poet he otherwise little resembles, Ammons skillfully deploys the line-break to advance (or at times to undercut) the meaning of his poem. Take the opening of "Gravelly Run":

> I don't know somehow it seems sufficient
> to see and hear whatever coming and going is,

The enjambment encourages us to consider the first line as a self-contained unit rather than as part of a longer clause, with the result that the *it* in "somehow it seems sufficient" acquires greater force.

Ammons's short poems are definitively lyric, a record of the encounters of the self with all that is foreign to the self in the universe. People turn up in his poems, though sometimes for no better reason than to illustrate the difference between a blabbermouth and a loudmouth (*Garbage*, in a passage not included here) or complain that the poet is "sneaky" ("Shot Glass"). Ammons knows himself too well to deny, as he puts it in "Poverty," that "it is not the same for / me as for others, that / being here to be here / with others is for others," not for him. He would much rather confer with the wind ("Mansion"), with an affable or sourpuss mountain ("Close-Up"), or even with a talkative willow ("Ballad") than with a cranky neighbor too absorbed in his errands to note the day's wondrous comet with "ten-million-mile tails" ("Dominion"). Ammons freely admits, in "The Put-Down Come On," that he is less interested in "contemporary / literature" than in letting his mind roam "where ideas of permanence / and transience fuse in a single body, ice, for example, / or a leaf." Or, for that matter, a weed. In "Reflective," one of his most celebrated short poems, there is artful symmetry and repetition: *weed* appears twice, sandwiching the three instances of *mirror*; notice, too, how much work the reiterated *in* does:

> I found a
> weed
> that had a
>
> mirror in it
> and that
> mirror
>
> looked in at
> a mirror
> in

me that
had a
weed in it

Ammons's friend Roald Hoffmann, a Nobel laureate in chemistry, says that "Reflective" is the "best poem in the English language written in words of no more than six letters." I like the specificity of this remark and would, in the same spirit, nominate "Their Sex Life" as the finest poem consisting of six words or less:

One failure on
Top of another

The symmetry here is fearful: there are three words per line, three words in the title; *One* and *on* flank *failure*; *failure* refers both to individuals and events; the capitalized *Top* makes us see the two lines themselves as the parallel lives of Mr. and Mrs. Failure. The key word is *failure*, but the sublime gesture is performed by the line break that separates *on* from *top*, and places *top* on the bottom.

In his long poems, Ammons figures out ways to extend and prolong the lyric impulse while assimilating the quotidian facts of his days as though they were trials and adventures and he a mild-mannered Odysseus, whose "story is how / a man comes home / from haunted / lands and transformations." Ammons, who made Ithaca, New York, his home for nearly forty years, told me once that he "came north and felt, as soon as people heard my accent, that I had to shoulder the whole burden of the South." And for other reasons as well, he writes in *Glare*, "sometimes I get the feeling I've never / lived here at all":

time collapses, so that nothing happened,
and I didn't exist, and existence

itself seems like a wayward temporizing,
an illusion nonexistence sometimes

stumbles into:

In long poems he characteristically seeks one image strong enough to sustain multiple perspectives: the earth as photographed from the moon in *Sphere*, a mound of rubbish off an interstate highway in Florida in *Garbage*. Garbage as the subject and theme of a poem was not without precedent in Ammons's work. The long poem "Summer Place," written in 1975 but not collected until *Brink Road* (1996), has some of Ammons's best riffs on trash:

> we should call this The Republic of Barrels of Trash:
> we could
> now be entering the bicentennial year of The United
> States of
> Barreling Trash: "pretty soon the people on welfare
> gone
>
> be richer than working people": The United States of
> Shining Garbage from Sea to Greasy Sea: the litter
> glitter: all that remains of free enterprise is if
>
> you fail you deserve it: the land of the hopeless case:
> the land of the biggest lobby:

The fascination with waste ("a waste is a terrible thing to mind"), trash ("I know trash, there's so much of it, democratic, / everything turns into it, and so few people want / it, there's a surplus of it, pick up free"), and garbage goes back to Ammons's habit, when typing *Tape for the Turn of the Year*, of letting the typed-up tape spiral into a wastepaper basket. The analogy with body processes presents itself, but perhaps the more pertinent analogy is with the image of the dirt at the close of Whitman's *Song of Myself*:

> I bequeath myself to the dirt to grow from the grass I
>   love,
> If you want me again look for me under your boot-
>   soles.

Like Whitman, Ammons believes with all his heart that —
as he writes in "Still" — there is "nothing lowly in the uni-
verse." And as for that bitter hug of mortality, as Whitman
calls it, Ammons can school himself to accept "the harmo-
nious / completion of the / drift," and even the "annihila-
tion" of consciousness, as he puts it in a poem strategically
entitled "Continuity." That is so because death imagined is
not an end but a continuation — and because our atoms
and molecules rejoin in other bodies, other lives. At the
end of "Still," Ammons stands in awe of his own epiphany:
all that he beholds is magnificent: "moss, beggar, weed, tick,
pine, self, magnificent / with being!" In a different mood
Ammons is not above telling the reader that "magnificent"
in the back woods of his childhood comes out "most-
maggie-went-a-fishing." Still, his homespun wit doesn't
diminish the visionary greatness of his poetry, the aim to
affirm the magnificence of creation, however lowly in ap-
pearance, however dark in design.

David Lehman
2005

So I Said I Am Ezra

So I said I am Ezra
and the wind whipped my throat
gaming for the sounds of my voice
   I listened to the wind
go over my head and up into the night
Turning to the sea I said
        I am Ezra
but there were no echoes from the waves
The words were swallowed up
   in the voice of the surf
or leaping over the swells
lost themselves oceanward
   Over the bleached and broken fields
I moved my feet and turning from the wind
   that ripped sheets of sand
   from the beach and threw them
   like seamists across the dunes
swayed as if the wind were taking me away
and said
        I am Ezra
As a word too much repeated
falls out of being
so I Ezra went out into the night
like a drift of sand
and splashed among the windy oats
that clutch the dunes
of unremembered seas

A Crippled Angel

A crippled angel bent in a scythe of grief
mourned in an empty lot
    Passing by I stopped
amused that immortality should grieve
and said
It must be exquisite

Smoke came out of the angel's ears
       the axles
    of slow handwheels of grief
and under the white lids of its eyes
bulged tears of purple light
Watching the agony diffuse in
       shapeless loss
I interposed a harp
    The atmosphere possessed it eagerly

and the angel
saying prayers for the things of time

let its fingers drop and burn
the lyric strings provoking wonder

Grief sounded like an ocean rose
       in bright clothes
and the fire
breaking out on the limbs rising
caught up the branching wings
    in a flurry of ascent

Taking a bow I shot transfixing
the angel midair
all miracle hanging fire
on rafters of the sky

Whose Timeless Reach

I Ezra the dying
portage of these deathless thoughts
stood on a hill in
the presence of the mountain
and said wisdom is
too wise for man it
is for gods and gods have little
use for it so I do not know what
to do with it
and animals use it only when
    their teeth start to fall and it
is too late to do anything
else but *be* wise and stay
out of the way
The eternal will not lie
down on any temporal hill
    The frozen mountain rose and broke
its tireless lecture of repose
and said death does
not take away it
ends giving halts bounty and
    Bounty I said thinking of ships
that I might take and helm right

out through space
dwarfing these safe harbors and
their values
taking the Way in whose timeless reach
cool thought unpunishable
by bones eternally glides

Hymn

I know if I find you I will have to leave the earth
and go on out
   over the sea marshes and the brant in bays
and over the hills of tall hickory
and over the crater lakes and canyons
and on up through the spheres of diminishing air
past the blackset noctilucent clouds
      where one wants to stop and look
way past all the light diffusions and bombardments
up farther than the loss of sight
   into the unseasonal undifferentiated empty stark

And I know if I find you I will have to stay with the earth
inspecting with thin tools and ground eyes
trusting the microvilli sporangia and simplest
   coelenterates
and praying for a nerve cell
with all the soul of my chemical reactions
and going right on down where the eye sees only traces

You are everywhere partial and entire
You are on the inside of everything and on the outside

I walk down the path down the hill where the sweetgum
has begun to ooze spring sap at the cut
and I see how the bark cracks and winds like no other bark
chasmal to my ant-soul running up and down
and if I find you I must go out deep into your
    far resolutions
and if I find you I must stay here with the separate leaves

Come Prima

I know
there is
perfection in the being
of my being,
that I am
holy in amness
as stars or
paperclips,

that the universe,
moving from void to void,
pours in and out
through me:

there is a point,
only itself,
that fills space,
an emptiness
that is plenitude:

a void that is all being,
a being that is void:

I am perfect:
the wind is perfect:
ditchwater, running, is perfect:
everything is:

I raise my hand

Mountain Liar

The mountains said they were
    tired of lying down
and wanted to know what
    I could do about
getting them off the ground

Well close your eyes I said
    and I'll see if I can
by seeing into your nature
    tell where you've been wronged
What do you think you want to do
    They said Oh fly

My hands are old
    and crippled keep no lyre
but if that is your true desire
    and conforms roughly
with your nature I said

    I don't see why
we shouldn't try
        to see something along that line

Hurry they said and snapped shut
        with rocky sounds their eyes
I closed mine and sure enough
        the whole range flew
gliding on interstellar ice

They shrieked with joy and peeked
        as if to see below
but saw me as before there
        foolish without my lyre
We haven't budged they said
        You wood

Gravelly Run

I don't know somehow it seems sufficient
to see and hear whatever coming and going is,
losing the self to the victory
    of stones and trees,
of bending sandpit lakes, crescent
round groves of dwarf pine:

for it is not so much to know the self
as to know it as it is known
    by galaxy and cedar cone,
as if birth had never found it
and death could never end it:

the swamp's slow water comes
down Gravelly Run fanning the long
    stone-held algal
hair and narrowing roils between
the shoulders of the highway bridge:

holly grows on the banks in the woods there,
and the cedars' gothic-clustered
    spires could make
green religion in winter bones:

so I look and reflect, but the air's glass
jail seals each thing in its entity:

no use to make any philosophies here:
    I see no
god in the holly, hear no song from
the snowbroken weeds: Hegel is not the winter
yellow in the pines: the sunlight has never
heard of trees: surrendered self among
    unwelcoming forms: stranger,
hoist your burdens, get on down the road.

Close-Up

Are all these stones
            yours
I said
and the mountain
pleased

but reluctant to
admit my praise could move it much

shook a little
and rained a windrow ring of stones
to show
that it was so

Stonefelled I got
up addled with dust

and shook
        myself
without much consequence

Obviously I said it doesn't pay
to get too
close up to
        greatness

and the mountain friendless wept
        and said
it couldn't help
itself

Mansion

So it came time
        for me to cede myself
and I chose
the wind
        to be delivered to

The wind was glad
        and said it needed all
the body
it could get
        to show its motions with

and wanted to know
        willingly as I hoped it would
if it could do
something in return
        to show its gratitude

When the tree of my bones
        rises from the skin I said
come and whirlwinding
stroll my dust
        around the plain

so I can see
        how the ocotillo does
and how saguaro-wren is
and when you fall
        with evening

fall with me here
     where we can watch
the closing up of day
and think how morning breaks

Guide

     You cannot come to unity and remain material:
in that perception is no perceiver:
  when you arrive
you have gone too far:
     at the Source you are in the mouth of Death:

you cannot
  turn around in
the Absolute: there are no entrances or exits
     no precipitations of forms
to use like tongs against the formless:
  no freedom to choose:

to be
     you have to stop not-being and break
off from *is* to *flowing* and
  this is the sin you weep and praise:
origin is your original sin:
     the return you long for will ease your guilt
and you will have your longing:

    the wind that is my guide said this: it
should know having
        given up everything to eternal being but
direction:

how I said can I be glad and sad: but a man goes
    from one foot to the other:
wisdom wisdom:
        to be glad and sad at once is also unity
and death:
    wisdom wisdom: a peachblossom blooms on a
        particular
tree on a particular day:
        unity cannot do anything in particular:

are these the thoughts you want me to think I said but
    the wind was gone and there was no more knowledge
        then.

Uh, Philosophy

I understand
    reading the modern philosophers
that truth is so much a method
        it's perfectly all
right for me to believe whatever
    I like or if I like,

nothing:
    I do not know that I care to be set that free:

I am they say
        at liberty to be
provisional, to operate
    expediently, do not have to commit myself

to imperturbables, outright
    legislations, hardfast rules:
they say I can
        prefer my truths,
whatever
    suits my blood,

blends with my proclivities, my temperament:
    I suppose they mean I've had more experience than I
            can
ever read about, taking in
        as I do
possibly a hundred sensations per second, conscious
    and unconscious,

and making a vegetal at least
    synthesis
from them all, so that
        philosophy is
a pry-pole, materialization,
    useful as a snowshovel when it snows:

something solid to knock people down with
    or back people up with:
I do not know that I care to be backed up in just that way:
        the philosophy gives clubs to

everyone, and I prefer disarmament:
 that is, I would rather relate

to the imperturbable objective
 than be the agent of
"possibly unsatisfactory eventualities":
  isn't anything plain true:
if I had something
 to conform to (without responsibility)

I wouldn't feel so hot and sticky:
 (but I must be moved by what I am moved by):
they do say, though, I must give some force to facts,
  must bend that way enough,
be in on the gist of "concrete observations,"
 must be pliant to the drift (roll with the knocks):

they say, too, I must halter my fancy
 mare
with these blinding limitations:
  I don't know that I can go along with that, either:
for though I've proved myself stupid by 33 years
 of getting nowhere,

I must nevertheless be given credit for the sense
  wherewith
 I decided never to set out:
what are facts if I can't line them up
  anyway I please
and have the freedom
 I refused I think in the beginning?

Epiphany

Like a single drop of rain,
    the wasp strikes
the windowpane; buzzes rapidly
away, disguising

error in urgent business:
    such is the
invisible, hard as glass,
unrenderable by the senses,

not known until stricken by:
    some talk that
there is safety in the visible,
the definite, the heard and felt,

pre-stressing the rational and
    calling out with
joy, like people far from death:
how puzzled they will be when

going headlong secure in "things"
    they strike the
intangible and break, lost,
unaccustomed to transparency, to

being without body, energy
    without image:
how they will be dealt
hard realizations, opaque as death.

Still

I said I will find what is lowly
    and put the roots of my identity
    down there:
each day I'll wake up

and find the lowly nearby,
    a handy focus and reminder,
a ready measure of my significance,
the voice by which I would be heard,
the wills, the kinds of selfishness
    I could
freely adopt as my own:

but though I have looked everywhere,
    I can find nothing
    to give myself to:
    everything is

magnificent with existence, is in
surfeit of glory:
nothing is diminished,
nothing has been diminished for me:

I said what is more lowly than the grass:
    ah, underneath,
    a ground-crust of dry-burnt moss:
    I looked at it closely
and said this can be my habitat: but
nestling in I

found
>   below the brown exterior
>   green mechanisms beyond intellect
awaiting resurrection in rain: so I got up

and ran saying there is nothing lowly in the universe:
I found a beggar:
he had stumps for legs: nobody was paying
him any attention: everybody went on by:
>   I nestled in and found his life:
there, love shook his body like a devastation:
I said
>   though I have looked everywhere
>   I can find nothing lowly
>   in the universe:

I whirled through transfigurations up and down,
transfigurations of size and shape and place:

>   at one sudden point came still,
>   stood in wonder:
moss, beggar, weed, tick, pine, self, magnificent
>   with being!

Corsons Inlet

I went for a walk over the dunes again this morning
to the sea,
then turned right along
   the surf
                    rounded a naked headland
                    and returned

   along the inlet shore:

it was muggy sunny, the wind from the sea steady and high,
crisp in the running sand,
     some breakthroughs of sun
   but after a bit

continuous overcast:

the walk liberating, I was released from forms,
from the perpendiculars,
     straight lines, blocks, boxes, binds
of thought
into the hues, shadings, rises, flowing bends and blends
      of sight:

                I allow myself eddies of meaning:
yield to a direction of significance
running
like a stream through the geography of my work:
   you can find

in my sayings
                    swerves of action
                    like the inlet's cutting edge:
          there are dunes of motion,
organizations of grass, white sandy paths of remembrance
in the overall wandering of mirroring mind:

but Overall is beyond me: is the sum of these events
I cannot draw, the ledger I cannot keep, the accounting
beyond the account:

in nature there are few sharp lines: there are areas of
primrose
          more or less dispersed;
disorderly orders of bayberry; between the rows
of dunes,
irregular swamps of reeds,
though not reeds alone, but grass, bayberry, yarrow,
          all . . .
predominantly reeds:

I have reached no conclusions, have erected no
          boundaries,
shutting out and shutting in, separating inside
          from outside: I have
          drawn no lines:
          as

manifold events of sand
change the dune's shape that will not be the same shape
tomorrow,

so I am willing to go along, to accept
the becoming
thought, to stake off no beginnings or ends, establish
        no walls:

by transitions the land falls from grassy dunes to creek
to undercreek: but there are no lines, though
    change in that transition is clear
    as any sharpness: but "sharpness" spread out,
allowed to occur over a wider range
than mental lines can keep:

the moon was full last night: today, low tide was low:
black shoals of mussels exposed to the risk
of air
and, earlier, of sun,
waved in and out with the waterline, waterline inexact,
caught always in the event of change:
    a young mottled gull stood free on the shoals
    and ate
to vomiting: another gull, squawking possession, cracked
    a crab,
picked out the entrails, swallowed the soft-shelled legs, a
    ruddy
turnstone running in to snatch leftover bits:

risk is full: every living thing in
siege: the demand is life, to keep life: the small
white blacklegged egret, how beautiful, quietly stalks
    and spears
        the shallows, darts to shore
            to stab—what? I couldn't

see against the black mudflats—a frightened
fiddler crab?

the news to my left over the dunes and
reeds and bayberry clumps was
        fall: thousands of tree swallows
        gathering for flight:
        an order held
        in constant change: a congregation
rich with entropy: nevertheless, separable, noticeable
        as one event,
                not chaos: preparations for
flight from winter,
cheet, cheet, cheet, cheet, wings rifling the green clumps,
beaks
at the bayberries
   a perception full of wind, flight, curve,
   sound:
   the possibility of rule as the sum of rulelessness:
the "field" of action
with moving, incalculable center:

in the smaller view, order tight with shape:
blue tiny flowers on a leafless weed: carapace of crab:
snail shell:
        pulsations of order
        in the bellies of minnows: orders swallowed,
broken down, transferred through membranes
to strengthen larger orders: but in the large view, no
lines or changeless shapes: the working in and out,
        together

and against, of millions of events: this,
           so that I make
           no form
           formlessness:

orders as summaries, as outcomes of actions override
or in some way result, not predictably (seeing me gain
the top of a dune,
the swallows
could take flight—some other fields of bayberry
           could enter fall
           berryless) and there is serenity:

           no arranged terror: no forcing of image, plan,
or thought:
no propaganda, no humbling of reality to precept:

terror pervades but is not arranged, all possibilities
of escape open: no route shut, except in
     the sudden loss of all routes:

           I see narrow orders, limited tightness, but will
not run to that easy victory:
           still around the looser, wider forces work:
           I will try
        to fasten into order enlarging grasps of disorder,
               widening
scope, but enjoying the freedom that
Scope eludes my grasp, that there is no finality of vision,
that I have perceived nothing completely,
           that tomorrow a new walk is a new walk.

Moment

He turned and
stood

in the moment's
height,

exhilaration
sucking him up,

shuddering and
lifting

him
jaw and bone

and he said
what

destruction am I
blessed by?

Reflective

I found a
weed
that had a

mirror in it
and that
mirror

looked in at
a mirror
in

me that
had a
weed in it

Communication

All day—I'm
surprised—the
orange tree, windy, sunny,
has said nothing:
nevertheless,
four ripe oranges have
dropped and several
dozen
given up a ghost of green.

Mountain Talk

I was going along a dusty highroad
when the mountain
across the way
turned me to its silence:
oh I said how come
I don't know your
massive symmetry and rest:
nevertheless, said the mountain,
would you want
to be
lodged here with
a changeless prospect, risen
to an unalterable view:
so I went on
counting my numberless fingers.

He Held Radical Light

He held radical light
as music in his skull: music
turned, as
over ridges immanences of evening light
rise, turned
back over the furrows of his brain
into the dark, shuddered,
shot out again
in long swaying swirls of sound:

reality had little weight in his transcendence
so he
had trouble keeping
his feet on the ground, was
terrified by that
and liked himself, and others, mostly
under roofs:
nevertheless, when the
light churned and changed

his head to music, nothing could keep him
off the mountains, his
head back, mouth working,
wrestling to say, to cut loose
from the high, unimaginable hook:
released, hidden from stars, he ate,
burped, said he was like any one
of us: demanded he
was like any one of us.

Poetics

I look for the way
things will turn
out spiralling from a center,
the shape
things will take to come forth in

so that the birch tree white
touched black at branches
will stand out
wind-glittering
totally its apparent self:

I look for the forms
things want to come as

from what black wells of possibility,
how a thing will
unfold:

not the shape on paper—though
that, too—but the
uninterfering means on paper:

not so much looking for the shape
as being available
to any shape that may be
summoning itself
through me
from the self not mine but ours.

6 Dec:

today I
decided to write
a long
   thin
   poem

     employing certain
classical considerations:
        this
part is called the pro-
logue: it has to do with
   the business of
   getting started:

   first the
   Muse
   must be acknowledged,
saluted, and implored:
I cannot
write
   without her help
   but when
her help comes it's
water from spring heights,
warmth and melting,
     stream
     inexhaustible:

I salute her, lady
of a hundred names—
    Inspiration
    Unconscious
    Apollo (on her man side)
    Parnassus (as her
            haunt)
Pierian spring (as
            the nature of her
                going)
    Hippocrene
    Pegasus:
most of all she's a
woman, maybe
a woman in us, who sets
fire to us, gives us no
            rest
            till her
        will's done:

because I've decided, the
Muse willing,
to do this foolish
        long
        thin
        poem, I
specially beg
assistance:
help me!
a fool who
plays with fool things:

so fools and play
can rise in the regard of
the people,
provide serious rest
and sweet engagement
to willing minds:

and the Muse be manifest:

I'm attracted to paper,
visualize
kitchen napkins
scribbled
with little masterpieces:
   so
it was natural for
me (in the House &
        Garden store one
night a couple weeks
ago) to contemplate
  this roll of
adding-machine tape, so
narrow, long,
unbroken, and to penetrate
  into some
  fool use for it: I
thought of the poem
then,
but not seriously: now,
two weeks
have gone by, and
    the Muse hasn't

rejected it,
seems caught up in the
      serious novelty:

I get weak in
the knees
(feel light in the head)
    when I look down
    and see
    how much footage is
tightly wound in that
roll: once started,
can I ever get
free
of the thing, get it in
and out of typewriter
and mind? one
rolled end, one
dangling, coiling end?

will the Muse fill it
up immediately and let me
loose? can my back
muscles last? my mind,
        can it be
        as long as
a tape
and unwind with it?

the Muse takes care of
    that: I do what I
can:

may this song be plain as
day, exact and bright!
no moonlight to loosen
    shrubs into
shapes that
never were: no dark
    nights to dissolve
    woods into one black
    depthless dimension:
may this song leave
darkness alone, deal
with what
light can win into clarity:

clarity & simplicity!

no muffled talk, fragments
of phrases, linked
without logical links,
strung
together in obscurities
supposed to reflect
density: it's
a wall
to obscure emptiness, the
talk of a posing man who
must talk
but who has nothing to
say: let this song
        make
complex things salient,

saliences clear, so
	there can be some
	understanding:

———

10 Jan:

today is windy as March
& sunny:
	a window whines like
boring bees:
	the outside lid
	of the exhaust fan
	in the kitchen
	flaps:
the wind's muffled weight
falls against the end of
the house:
whipping branches
	in whistling trees:

	we turn away from
	galaxies
to the warm knot
in the dark:

	somehow in taking
	pleasure
		from yr body,
	I have given you
	my heart:

I care now
more for you than for
the pleasure you give
me:
    you, your total
self, my anchorage:
the universe shifts its
center:
it turns about you:
    who are you?
    will you destroy
    me?

went to a
party last
night:
& the living room was
large:
the guests sat around
the walls
in a periphery of beads:
some beads clustered into
groups:
    but it was too far
    to cast a line
    across the room's
vacant center:
lack of unity:
disintegration overall
    with random
    integrations:

        fun, tho: beads
shift,
regrouping the periphery:
combinations:

my plants are in full sun
now,
the chloroplasts
    are working round the
    peripheries of cells:

        look!
        there's the red
        ink!
        rising from the
        floor:

Muse, I've done the best
I could:
    sometimes you ran out
    on me
    & sometimes I ran out
    on you:

    I know you better now:
    you've come closer:
        will you
        confer the high
grace of your touch?
come & live enduring with

me:
        I'll be faithful:
        I won't trick you:
        I'll give you all
        I've got:
        bestow tendance &
concern:

help me to surrender
myself:
        I'll be the
        fingers & keys
of your song:
        I'll ask nothing
        but the sound
of yr voice:

reader, we've been thru
a lot together:
        who are you?
        where will you go
        now?

                ***

coughed a lot last night:
round
4:20 a.m. got up &
        took a shot of
        brandy:

        numbed the tickle
some:
        slept better:

        just had lunch:
cold baked ham:
coffee: chocolate fudge
        cookie:

        last night had duck
(Bobby's favorite) at
 Mary's: conversation:
                hearing people
talk, how marvelous:
I'm alone too much: get
to think
other people
        aren't people:

the 200-inch glass
shows a
billion-billion galaxies:
what is God
        to this grain of sand:

        dispersions:
        it's as brave to accept
boundaries,
turn to the center given,
& do the best you can:

think of other
people: devise some
way of living
together:

get some fun out of life:

how about the one who sez:
   it's too late
   for me to start: I
   haven't got anywhere:
   I can't get anywhere:

      how do the hopeless
      get some fun out of
      life?

      apes get
something out of life:
they don't ask what is:
            bamboo shoots,
tender, cool:
they have a head man:
   they pair off
   & raise babies:
   they defend:
   they sometimes rest in

clearings
and groom themselves
   in sunlight:

have our minds taken us too
far, out of nature, out of
complete acceptance?

we haven't remembered our
bodies:
   let's touch, patiently,
   thoroughly: beyond
   vanity:

but for all our trouble
with the mind,
look what it's done:
   a fact at a time:
   a little here (there's
the red ink
turned into the light!)
a little there:
let's be patient: much
remains
to be known: there may
come
re-evaluation:
    if we don't have
    the truth, we've
      shed
      thousands of errors:

      haven't seen the
      jay:
      a sparrowhawk

can stand still
in a high wind, too:

coming home:
       how does one come
       home:

        self-acceptance:
        reconciliation,
a way of
going along with this
world as it is:

nothing ideal: not as
you'd have it:
testing, feeling the way:
   ready to
   readjust, to make
            amends:

self, not as you would
have it:
   nevertheless, take
   it:
     do the best you
     can with it:

I wrote about these
days
the way life gave them:
   I didn't know

beforehand what I
wd write,
whether I'd meet
anything new: I
showed that I'm sometimes
blank & abstract,
sometimes blessed with
song: sometimes
silly, vapid, serious,
angry, despairing:
        ideally, I'd
        be like a short poem:
        that's a fine way
        to be: a poem at a
time: but all day
life itself is bending,
weaving, changing,
adapting, failing,
        succeeding:

        I've given
you my
emptiness: it may
not be unlike
        your emptiness:
        in voyages, there
        are wide reaches
        of water
        with no islands:

I've given you the
interstices: the
   space between
   electrons:
   I've given you
   the dull days
when turning & turning
revealed nothing:
I've given you the
sky,
uninterrupted by moon,
bird, or cloud:
        I've given
you long
uninteresting walks
so you could experience
vacancy:

old castles, carnivals,
ditchbanks,
   bridges, ponds,
     steel mills,
     cities: so many
interesting tours:

the roll has lifted
from the floor &
our journey is done:
thank you
for coming: thank
you for coming along:

the sun's bright:
the wind rocks the
    naked trees:
    so long:

Dominion

I said
Mr. Schafer
did you get up see the comet:

and
he said
Oh no
let it go by, I don't care:

he has leaves to rake
and the
plunger on his washing machine isn't working right:

he's not amused
by ten-million-mile tails
or any million-mile-an-hour
universal swoosh

or
frozen gases
lit by disturbances

across our
solar arcs

Cascadilla Falls

I went down by Cascadilla
Falls this
evening, the
stream below the falls,
and picked up a
handsized stone
kidney-shaped, testicular, and

thought all its motions into it,
the 800 mph earth spin,
the 190-million-mile yearly
displacement around the sun,
the overriding
grand
haul

of the galaxy with the 30,000
mph of where
the sun's going:
thought all the interweaving
motions
into myself: dropped

the stone to dead rest:
the stream from other motions
broke
rushing over it:
shelterless,
I turned

to the sky and stood still:
Oh
I do
not know where I am going
that I can live my life
by this single creek.

Reversal

The mt in my head surpasses you
I said

becomes at the base
more nearly incalculable with

bush
more divisive with suckers and roots

and at the peak
far less visible

plumed and misty
opening from unfinal rock to air:

arrogance arrogance
the mt said

the wind in your days
accounts for this arrogance

Positions

I can tell you what I need is for
somebody to asseverate I'm a poet
and in an embroilment and warfare of onrushing words
   heightened by opposing views
to maintain I lie down to no man in
the character and thrust of my speech
and that everybody who is neglecting me far
   though it be, indeed, from his mind
is incurring a guilt complex
he'll have to reckon with later on
and suffer over (I am likely to be
recalcitrant with leniency):
what I need I mean is a champion or even
   a host of champions,
a phalanx of enthusiasts, driving a spearhead
or one or two of those big amphibian trucks
through the peopled ocean of my neglect:
I mean I don't want to sound fancy but
what I could use at the moment is
a little destruction perpetrated in my favor.

Correction

The burdens of the world
on my back
lighten the world
not a whit while
removing them greatly
decreases my specific
gravity

Mirrorment

Birds are flowers flying
and flowers perched birds.

The Put-Down Come On

You would think I'd be a specialist in contemporary
literature: novels, short stories, books of poetry,
my friends write many of them: I don't read much
and some drinks are too strong for me: my empty-
        headed

contemplation is still where the ideas of permanence
and transience fuse in a single body, ice, for example,
or a leaf: green pushes white up the slope: a maple
leaf gets the wobbles in a light wind and comes loose

half-ready: where what has always happened and what
has never happened before seem for an instant reconciled:
that takes up most of my time and keeps me uninformed:
but the slope, after maybe a thousand years, may spill

and the ice have a very different look withdrawing into
the lofts of cold: only a little of that kind of
thinking flashes through: but turning the permanent also
into the transient takes up all the time that's left.

Play

Nothing's going to become of anyone
except death:
   therefore: it's okay
to yearn
too high:
the grave accommodates
swell rambunctiousness &

ruin's not
compromised by magnificence:

that cut-off point
liberates us to the

common disaster: so
   pick a perch—
apple branch for example in bloom—
tune up
and

drill imagination right through necessity:
it's all right:
it's been taken care of:

is allowed, considering

Working Still

I can't think of a thing to uphold:
the carborundum plant snows
sift-scum on the slick, outgoing river
and along the avenues car wheels

float in a small powder: my made-up
mind idles like a pyramid: oxides
"under proper atmospheric conditions" become
acids and rain a fine broad bleaching:

man's a plant parasite: so I drop
down to the exchange, $CO_2 \leftrightarrow O_2$, and
find dread there, just dread: too
much care fuddles me dull:

beef hormones bloom monstrous
with tenderness:
but I won't take up the scaring cause
and can't think of a thing to uphold.

The Unifying Principle

Ramshackles, archipelagoes, loose constellations
are less fierce, subsidiary centers, with the
attenuations of interstices, roughing the salience,

jarring the outbreak of too insistent commonalty:
a board, for example, not surrendering the rectitude
of its corners, the island of the oaks an

admonishment to pines, underfigurings (as of the Bear)
that take identity on: this motion is against
the grinding oneness of seas, hallows distinction

into the specific: but less lovely, too, for how
is the mass to be amassed, by what sanction
neighbor touch neighbor, island bear resemblance,

how are distinction's hard lines to be dissolved
(and preserved): what may all the people turn to,
the old letters, the shaped, characteristic peak

generations of minds have deflected and kept:
a particular tread that sometimes unweaves, taking
more shape on, into dance: much must be

tolerated as out of timbre, out of step, as being not
in its time or mood (the hiatus of the unconcerned)
and much room provided for the wretched to find caves

to ponder way off in: what then can lift the people
and only when they choose to rise or what can make
them want to rise, though business prevents: the

unifying principle will be a
phrase shared, an old cedar long known, general
wind-shapes in a usual sand: those objects single,

single enough to be uninterfering, multiple by
the piling on of shared sight, touch, saying:
when it's found the people live the small wraths of ease.

Triphammer Bridge

I wonder what to mean by *sanctuary*, if a real or
apprehended place, as of a bell rung in a gold
surround, or as of silver roads along the beaches

of clouds seas don't break or black mountains
overspill; jail: ice here's shapelier than anything,
on the eaves massive, jawed along gorge ledges, solid

in the plastic blue boat fall left water in: if I
think the bitterest thing I can think of that seems like
reality, slickened back, hard, shocked by rip-high wind:

sanctuary, sanctuary, I say it over and over and the
word's sound is the one place to dwell: that's it, just
the sound, and the imagination of the sound—a place.

The City Limits

When you consider the radiance, that it does not
          withhold
itself but pours its abundance without selection into
          every
nook and cranny not overhung or hidden; when you
          consider

that birds' bones make no awful noise against the light
    but
lie low in the light as in a high testimony; when you
    consider
the radiance, that it will look into the guiltiest

swervings of the weaving heart and bear itself upon
    them,
not flinching into disguise or darkening; when you
    consider
the abundance of such resource as illuminates the glow-
    blue

bodies and gold-skeined wings of flies swarming the
    dumped
guts of a natural slaughter or the coil of shit and in no
way winces from its storms of generosity; when you
    consider

that air or vacuum, snow or shale, squid or wolf, rose or
    lichen,
each is accepted into as much light as it will take, then
the heart moves roomier, the man stands and looks
    about, the

leaf does not increase itself above the grass, and the dark
work of the deepest cells is of a tune with May bushes
and fear lit by the breadth of such calmly turns to praise.

For Harold Bloom

I went to the summit and stood in the high nakedness:
the wind tore about this
way and that in confusion and its speech could not
get through to me nor could I address it:
still I said as if to the alien in myself
    I do not speak to the wind now:
for having been brought this far by nature I have been
brought out of nature
and nothing here shows me the image of myself:
for the word *tree* I have been shown a tree
and for the word *rock* I have been shown a rock,
for stream, for cloud, for star
this place has provided firm implication and answering
    but where here is the image for *longing*:
so I touched the rocks, their interesting crusts:
I flaked the bark of stunt-fir:
I looked into space and into the sun
and nothing answered my word *longing*:
    goodbye, I said, goodbye, nature so grand and
reticent, your tongues are healed up into their own
element
and as you have shut up you have shut me out: I am
as foreign here as if I had landed, a visitor:
so I went back down and gathered mud
and with my hands made an image for *longing*:
    I took the image to the summit: first
I set it here, on the top rock, but it completed
nothing: then I set it there among the tiny firs
but it would not fit:

so I returned to the city and built a house to set
the image in
and men came into my house and said
    that is an image for *longing*
and nothing will ever be the same again

FROM **Sphere: The Form of a Motion**

1

The sexual basis of all things rare is really apparent
and fools crop up where angels are mere disguises:
a penetrating eye (insight), a penetrating tongue (ah),

a penetrating penis and withal a penetrating mind,
integration's consummation: a com- or intermingling of
        parts,
heterocosm joyous, opposite motions away and toward

along a common line, the in-depth knowledge (a dilly),
the concentration and projection (firmly energized) and
the ecstasy, the pay off, the play out, the expended

nexus nodding, the flurry, cell spray, finish, the
haploid hungering after the diploid condition: the
        reconciler
of opposites, commencement, proliferation, ontogeny:

2

often those who are not good for much else turn to
        thought

and it's just great, part of the grand possibility, that
thought is there to turn to: camouflagy thought flushed

out of the bush, seen vaguely as potential form, and
pursued, pursued and perceived, declared: the savored
form, the known possession, knowledge carnal
    knowledge:

the seizure, the satiation: the heavy jaguar takes the
burro down for a foreleg or so: then, the lighter,
though still heavy, vultures pull and gulp: then, the

tight-bodied black crows peck and scratch: then ants
come out and run around the structure, picking bits:
finally, least bacteria boil the last grease mild:

3

so the lessening transformers arrive at the subtle
    condition
fine, the spiritual burro braying free, overwhelming
the hairy, and so must we all approach the fine, our

skinny house perpetual, where in total diminishment we
    will
last, elemental and irreducible, the matter of the universe:
slosh, slosh: vulnerability is merely intermediate: beyond

the autopsy and the worm, the blood cell, protein,
    amino acid,
the nervous atom spins and shines unsmirched: the total,
necessary arrival, the final victory, utterly the total loss:

we're haplessly one way the wrong way on the runway:
conglomerates, tongues or eyes or heel strings that
keep us, won't keep: we want to change without
    changing

4

out of change: actually, the imagination works pretty
diagrammatically into paradigm so one can "see things":
and then talk fairly tirelessly without going astray or

asunder: for me, for example, the one-many problem
    figures
out as an isoceles triangle (base: diversity and peak:
    unity)
or, even, equilateral, some rigor of rising: and this is

not to be distinguished from the center-periphery
    thing, in
that if you cut out a piece of pie from the center-
    periphery
circle, you have a triangle, a little rocky, but if you

cut off the arc, it sits up good, as (peak: center: unity)
and (base: periphery: diversity): actually, one could go
    even
so far as (peak: center: symbol: abstraction), etc., and the
    other:

5

this works in the bedrock, too, or undifferentiated gas:
one feels up the two legs of the possibility and, ever
tightening and steered, rises to the crux, to find

there the whole mystery, the lush squeeze, the centering
and prolongation: so much so that the final stone
never locks the peak but inlet: outlet opens unfolding

into nothingness's complete possibility, the strangling
through into the darkness of futurity: it is hard at this
point to avoid some feeling, however abstract the
        circumstance:

if one can get far enough this way where imagination
and flesh strive together in shocking splendors, one can
forget that sensibility is sometimes dissociated and
        come:

6
I wouldn't be surprised if the radiance we talk about isn't
that part of the structureless lust that rising from the
depths gets by all the mechanisms of mediation and, left
        over,

feels like religion, the heights visited; that is, the route
from energy to energy without frigging, an untainted
        source
with an untainted end: when the professor rises to
        require

structure in the compositions, he invokes a woman: he
        wants
shapeliness intact, figure shown forth: dirty old
man hawking order and clarity: but if he would not

be dark, what a brightness! though I am not enjoying the
first day of spring very much, it is not with me as it is
with my friend George, spending his first spring in the
    grave:

———

151

harmonies (in my magnum hokum) I would speak of,
    though
chiefly as calling attention to neglected aspects of fairly
common, at least overreaching, experience: with
    considerable

rasping along the edges, bulgings of boundaries, we made
and tamed into play each of these States: if the States
kept falling into lesser clusters about lesser points of

focus (and then the long division, so costly), still we
checked and balanced and, incorporating as much sin as
    grace
with each holding, kept the mobile afloat, together, each

dangle with good range to dip and rise and convey itself
roundly with windy happenstance, communicating,
    though, its
position throughout the network and receiving from the
    sums

of the network just adjustments: yes, we got it all together,
ocean to ocean, high temperate to low temperate, and
    took
in so much multiplicity that what we hold person to
    person

in common exists only in the high levels of constitution or
out to the neighbor's fence, an extreme, an extreme pity,
with little consolation in the middle after all: still,

it holds and moves within the established rigors: now,
    with
the same rasping and groaning, we try to put the nations
    and
communities of nations together and there, too, only by

joining tenuous extremes, asserting the dignity of the
    single
person above united nations: we pray this may succeed
    and
correct much evil in the dark edges of dislocation and

distraction: lately, we've left out the high ranges of
    music,
the planetary, from our response, though the one sun is
    here
as usual and the planets continue to obey holy roads: the

galaxy is here, nearly too much to speak of, sagely and
tremendously observing its rotation: we do have
        something to
tune in with and move toward: not homogeneous
        pudding but

united differences, surface differences expressing the
        common,
underlying hope and fate of each person and people, a
        gathering
into one place of multiple dissimilarity, each culture to its

own cloth and style and tongue and gait, each culture,
        like
the earth itself with commonlode center and variable
        surface,
designed-out to the exact limit of ramification, to
        discrete

154

expression into the visible, specific congruence of form
        and
matter, energy moving into the clarification of each face,
        hand,
ear, mouth, eye, billions: still with the sense of the
        continuous

running through and staying all the discretions,
        differences
diminished into the common tide of feelings, so that
        difference

cannot harden into aggression or hate fail to move with
    the

ongoing, the differences not submerged but resting clear
    at
the surface, as the surface, and not rising above the
    surface
so as to become more visible and edgy than the
    continuum:

a united, capable poem, a united, capable mind, a united
    capable
nation, and a united nations! capable, flexible, yielding,
accommodating, seeking the good of all in the good of
    each:

155
to float the orb or suggest the orb is floating: and, with
    the
mind thereto attached, to float free: the orb floats, a
    bluegreen
wonder: so to touch the structures as to free them into
    rafts

that reveal the tide: many rafts to ride and the tides
    make a
place to go: let's go and regard the structures, the six-
    starred
easter lily, the beans feeling up the stakes: we're gliding:
    we

are gliding: ask the astronomer, if you don't believe it: but

motion as a summary of time and space is gliding us: for
    a while,

we may ride such forces: then, we must get off: but now
    this

beats any amusement park by the shore: our Ferris
    wheel, what a

wheel: our roller coaster, what mathematics of stoop and
    climb: sew

my name on my cap: we're clear: we're ourselves: we're
    sailing.

Ballad

I want to know the unity in all things and the difference
between one thing and another
   I said to the willow
and asked what it wanted to know: the willow said it
wanted to know how to get rid of the wateroak
that was throwing it into shade every afternoon at
     4 o'clock: that is a real problem I said I suppose
and the willow, once started, went right on saying
I can't take you for a friend because while you must
be interested in willowness, which you could find
   nowhere better than right here,
     I'll bet you're just as interested in wateroakness
which you can find in a pure form right over there,
a pure form of evil and death to me:

I know I said I want to be friends with you both but the
willow sloughed into a deep grief
and said
if you could just tie back some of those oak branches
until I can get a little closer to mastering that domain
of space up there—see it? how empty it is
and how full of light:
    why I said don't I ask the wateroak if he would mind
withholding himself until you're more nearly even: after
all I said you are both trees and you both need water and
light and space to unfold into, surely the wateroak will
understand that commonness:
  not so you could tell it, said the willow:
    that I said is cynical and uncooperative: what could
you give the wateroak in return for his withholding:
what could I give him, said the willow, nothing
that he hasn't already taken:
  well, I said, but does he know about the unity in
all things, does he understand that all things have a
common source and end: if he could be made
to see that rather deeply, don't you think he might give
    you a little way:
  no said the willow he'd be afraid I would take all:
would you I said:
or would you, should the need come, give him a little
    way
back:
    I would said the willow but my need is greater than
his
and the trade would not be fair:

maybe not I said but let's approach him with our
        powerful
concept that all things are in all
    and see if he will be moved

One Must Recall as One Mourns the Dead

One must recall as one mourns the dead
to mourn the dead and so not mourn too much

thinking how deprived away the dead lie
from the gold and red of our rapt wishes

and not mourn the dead too much who having
broken at the lip the nonesuch

bubble oblivion, the cold grape of ease at
last in whose range no further

ravages afflict the bones, no more
fires flash through the flarings of dreams

do not mourn the dead too much who bear no
knowledge, have no need or fear of pain,

and who never again must see death
come upon what does not wish to die

The Perfect Journey Is

The perfect journey is
no need to go

another nothingly clear day and
I went
to walk between the pine
colonnades
up the road on the hill and there
hill-high in dry cold
I saw the weaves of glitterment
airborne, so fine,
the breeze sifting
figurations from the snow
reservoirs of the boughs

You Can't Imitate

You can't imitate
anybody really
and the extent
to which
you can't is
enough originality

the extent to
which you can't
imitate anyone
really is enough
originality

one gains
with immortality
a lasting
tomb

after another blow
I pick up
loose wood
under the elm,

                              hard branches, the
                              skinny bones
                              of a flesh
if you caught a   left
dusk-glimpse   that was leaves
as a first seeing
of the thin-tapering
hemlocks (a row   ringneck &
of raving beauties)   redwing
you'd think they'd,   (redneck &
waggled and whipped,   ringwing)
worn off in the
wind that way

Stevens, you should be here
now with the ringnecks
and rigorous rednecks
and the green billows
of grass with drained
hunks of black-old
snow floating in them
and the ringnecks
stirred by a nosey dog
racing into the thickets!
if you could hear the
brook like a bear breaking
through the thicket

(the thicket floor
a manuscript patches
of snow illuminate)

yours truly
yours treely

    "live unknown" is
    no fun unless
    you have to work at it

why kill
yourself when
you can
die
without
your help   trees fall to
            the wind
            and falls'
            murmuring
            trees the wind
the comet mingling
with us this
week (a
windy week)
will
be back in
fifty
thousand years   the grave may
                not be its
                goal but that's
                where it lands
the world's too serious
to take seriously &
too funny to take lightly   faint &
                        fall over

Old Milling

say to the race
your run's
run its race

say to the run
your race's
race's run

Some Nights I Go Out to Piss

Some nights I go out to piss
among the big black scary shrubs:
the tinkling stars
don't seem to mind:

cruddy crude   stars & stones
 ruddy rude   silent & naked

odd that where no one is to have
anything, not even his
own life,
    having is the game:
that where no one is to win
but indeed lose losing
    itself
    the game is winning:
and where not a single love,
mother-child, lover-girl, man-son,

is to hold,
    love settles in:
odd, odd that as the days go
by so rich, so lost, one fool, trying to save it,
wastes the day

contradiction is a center
turning around makes
another place to go

nasty century! whose
enlightenment
fills the air with smoke,
darkens the day

In Memoriam
Mae Noblitt

This is just a place:
we go around, distanced,
yearly in a star's

atmosphere, turning
daily into and out of
direct light and

slanting through the
quadrant seasons: deep
space begins at our

heels, nearly rousing
us loose: we look up
or out so high, sight's

silk almost draws us away:
this is just a place:
currents worry themselves

coiled and free in airs
and oceans: water picks
up mineral shadow and

plasm into billions of
designs, frames: trees,
grains, bacteria: but

is love a reality we
made here ourselves—
and grief—did we design

that—or do these,
like currents, whine
in and out among us merely

as we arrive and go:
this is just a place:
the reality we agree with,

that agrees with us,
outbounding this, arrives
to touch, joining with

us from far away:
our home which defines
us is elsewhere but not

so far away we have
forgotten it:
this is just a place.

Easter Morning

I have a life that did not become,
that turned aside and stopped,
astonished:
I hold it in me like a pregnancy or
as on my lap a child
not to grow or grow old but dwell on

it is to his grave I most
frequently return and return
to ask what is wrong, what was
wrong, to see it all by
the light of a different necessity
but the grave will not heal
and the child,
stirring, must share my grave
with me, an old man having
gotten by on what was left

when I go back to my home country in these
fresh far-away days, it's convenient to visit

everybody, aunts and uncles, those who used to say,
look how he's shooting up, and the
trinket aunts who always had a little
something in their pocketbooks, cinnamon bark
or a penny or nickel, and uncles who
were the rumored fathers of cousins
who whispered of them as of great, if
troubled, presences, and school
teachers, just about everybody older
(and some younger) collected in one place
waiting, particularly, but not for
me, mother and father there, too, and others
close, close as burrowing
under skin, all in the graveyard
assembled, done for, the world they
used to wield, have trouble and joy
in, gone

the child in me that could not become
was not ready for others to go,
to go on into change, blessings and
horrors, but stands there by the road
where the mishap occurred, crying out for
help, come and fix this or we
can't get by, but the great ones who
were to return, they could not or did
not hear and went on in a flurry and
now, I say in the graveyard, here
lies the flurry, now it can't come
back with help or helpful asides, now
we all buy the bitter

incompletions, pick up the knots of
horror, silently raving, and go on
crashing into empty ends not
completions, not rondures the fullness
has come into and spent itself from

I stand on the stump
of a child, whether myself
or my little brother who died, and
yell as far as I can, I cannot leave this place, for
for me it is the dearest and the worst,
it is life nearest to life which is
life lost: it is my place where
I must stand and fail,
calling attention with tears
to the branches not lofting
boughs into space, to the barren
air that holds the world that was my world

though the incompletions
(& completions) burn out
standing in the flash high-burn
momentary structure of ash, still it
is a picture-book, letter-perfect
Easter morning: I have been for a
walk: the wind is tranquil: the brook
works without flashing in an abundant
tranquility: the birds are lively with
voice: I saw something I had
never seen before: two great birds,
maybe eagles, blackwinged, whitenecked

and -headed, came from the south oaring
the great wings steadily; they went
directly over me, high up, and kept on
due north: but then one bird,
the one behind, veered a little to the
left and the other bird kept on seeming
not to notice for a minute: the first
began to circle as if looking for
something, coasting, resting its wings
on the down side of some of the circles:
the other bird came back and they both
circled, looking perhaps for a draft;
they turned a few more times, possibly
rising—at least, clearly resting—
then flew on falling into distance till
they broke across the local bush and
trees: it was a sight of bountiful
majesty and integrity: the having
patterns and routes, breaking
from them to explore other patterns or
better ways to routes, and then the
return: a dance sacred as the sap in
the trees, permanent in its descriptions
as the ripples round the brook's
ripplestone: fresh as this particular
flood of burn breaking across us now
from the sun.

Sunday at McDonald's

In the bleak land of foreverness no
one lives but only, crushed and buffeted,
now: now, now, now every star glints

perishing while now slides under and
away, slippery as light, time-vapor:
what can butterflies do or clear-eyed

babies gumming french fries—nature
is holding them, somehow, veering them
off into growth holdings, forms

brought to peaks of splendor, sharp
energies burring into each other to
set off new progressions through the

rustle and mix, rot and slush: is
this the way it is: sometimes a man
will stand up, clear and settled as

a bright day, and seem to look through
the longest times and roilings to
the still, star-bending, fixed ahead.

Poverty

I'm walking home from, what,
a thousandth walk this year
along the same macadam's edge
(pebbly) the ragweed rank
but not blooming yet,
a rose cloud passed to the
east that against sundown would be
blue-gray, the moon up nearly
full, splintering
through the tips of street pine,
and the hermit lark downhill
in a long glade cutting
spirals of musical ice, and I
realize that it is not the same for
me as for others, that
being here to be here
with others is for others.

Immoderation

If something is too
big, enlarging it
may correct it:

a skinny thing
acquires great force
pushed next to nothing.

The Role of Society in the Artist

Society sent me this invitation to go to
hell and
delighted not to be overlooked I thought

I could make arrangements to accommodate
it and went off
where, however, I

did the burning by myself, developing
fortunately some fairly thick shields
against blazing and some games

one of which was verse by which I used
illusion to put the flames out,
turning flares into mirrors

of seeming: society
attracted to this bedazzlement wanted me
to acknowledge how it had been

largely responsible and I said oh yes it gave
me the language by which to send me
clear invitations and society

designated me of social value and lifted me
out of hell so I could better share
paradisal paradigms with it

and it said isn't it generous
of society to let you walk here
far from hell—society does this because

it likes your keen sense of acquired sight
& word: how wonderful of you to say so, I said,
and took some of whatever was being

passed around but every night went out
into the forest to spew fire
that blazoned tree trunks and set

stumps afire and society found me out there
& warmed itself and said it liked my unconventional
verses best & I invited society to go to hell

Shit List; or,
Omnium-gatherum of Diversity into Unity

You'll rejoice at how many kinds of shit there are:
gosling shit (which J. Williams said something
was as green as), fish shit (the generality), trout

shit, rainbow trout shit (for the nice), mullet shit,
sand dab shit, casual sloth shit, elephant shit
(awesome as process or payload), wildebeest shit,

horse shit (a favorite), caterpillar shit (so many dark
kinds, neatly pelleted as mint seed), baby rhinoceros
shit, splashy jaybird shit, mockingbird shit

(dive-bombed with the aim of song), robin shit that
oozes white down lawnchairs or down roots under roosts,
chicken shit and chicken mite shit, pelican shit, gannet

shit (wholesome guano), fly shit (periodic), cockatoo
shit, dog shit (past catalog or assimilation),
cricket shit, elk (high plains) shit, and

tiny scribbled little shrew shit, whale shit (what
a sight, deep assumption), mandril shit (blazing
blast off), weasel shit (wiles' waste), gazelle shit,

magpie shit (total protein), tiger shit (too acid
to contemplate), moray eel and manta ray shit, eerie
shark shit, earthworm shit (a soilure), crab shit,

wolf shit upon the germicidal ice, snake shit, giraffe
shit that accelerates, secretary bird shit, turtle
shit suspension invites, remora shit slightly in

advance of the shark shit, hornet shit (difficult to
assess), camel shit that slaps the ghastly dry
siliceous, frog shit, beetle shit, bat shit (the

marmoreal), contemptible cat shit, penguin shit,
hermit crab shit, prairie hen shit, cougar shit, eagle
shit (high totem stuff), buffalo shit (hardly less

lofty), otter shit, beaver shit (from the animal of
alluvial dreams)—a vast ordure is a broken down
cloaca—macaw shit, alligator shit (that floats the Nile

along), louse shit, macaque, koala, and coati shit,
antelope shit, chuck-will's-widow shit, alpaca shit
(very high stuff), gooney bird shit, chigger shit, bull

shit (the classic), caribou shit, rasbora, python, and
razorbill shit, scorpion shit, man shit, laswing
fly larva shit, chipmunk shit, other-worldly wallaby

shit, gopher shit (or broke), platypus shit, aardvark
shit, spider shit, kangaroo and peccary shit, guanaco
shit, dolphin shit, aphid shit, baboon shit (that leopards

induce), albatross shit, red-headed woodpecker (nine
inches long) shit, tern shit, hedgehog shit, panda shit,
seahorse shit, and the shit of the wasteful gallinule.

Immortality

The double lanceolate
needlelike
hemlock leaf

will, falling, catch on
a twitch of old
worm-silk

and, like a fall worm,
dingledangle breezy
all day in the noose

The Fairly High Assimilation Rag

Plato derives the many from the one and Aristotle
the one from the many, and these two together give
the flip-flop sides of a dynamics too

one and two for easy entry or exit: parallel with
that philosophical goes the religious, in which
the One devolves and assuages into the fiats and

specifications of specialized deities, into poly-
theism, and in which the many accumulate up, dissolving
their intense boundaries into the blurs and glows

and finally on up of course to the absolute absence
and clarity of the total presence, One unspeakable,
monotheism: answering back and forth with heat

exchangers and mitochondria and other particulars in
and out of focus is the hierarchy, the one:many
mechanism we everywhere seek and renounce: like

a mobile in which the wires are, though the only
means of support, hardly visible and where the bright
parts at liberty to play seem to be the reason for it all—

like that we seek the rigorous, tense, thin dispositions
that allow the colorful personal feelings of free,
unoriented, singular family, all the way to the play

out of each his individual set of bones and wishes:
oh yes: the one:many's the metaphysical (and discrete)
wherein we entertain systems high and low, sharp and

fuzzy, radiant and drained, pertaining to most anything:
still, we don't look to the wiring for immediate
help or hope as often as to the family vacations,

and we are hurt by nothing so much as children's
chances, their terrible uprisings and misleading
procedures: society will wind and unwind but we may

or may not have a nice weekend depending on whether
or not we have been divorced or have enough booze
to last through Sunday: the particulars are so

close they are nobody else's business (largely)
whereas everybody does a little for the hierarchy
without which we would not know which way to turn.

I Could Not Be Here At All

Momentous and trivial, I
walk along the lake cliff
and look north where the lake
curls to a wisp through the hills

and say as if to the lake,
I'm here, too,
and to the winter storm centered
gnarl-black over the west bank,

I nearly call out, it's me, I'm here:
the wind-fined
snow nicks
my face, mists my lashes

and the sun, not dwindling me, goes
on down behind the storm and the reed
withes' wind doesn't whistle, brother! brother!
and no person comes.

Autonomy

I am living without you because
    of a terror, a farfetched
notion that I
can't live without you

which I must narrow down & quell,
    for how can I live
worthy of you, in the
freedom of your limber engagements,

in the casual uptakes of your
    sweetest compliances
if stricken in your presence
by what your absence stills:

to have you, I school myself
    to let you go; how terrible
to buy that absence
before the fragrance of any presence comes:

but though I am living without
   you, surely
I can't live
without you: the thought of

you hauls my heavy
   body up,
floats me around,
gives my motions point, just the thought.

Their Sex Life

One failure on
Top of another

For Louise and Tom Gossett

After a creek
drink
the goldfinch
lights in

the bank willow
which
drops the brook
a yellow leaf.

what are we to think of the waste, though: the
sugarmaple seeds on the blacktop are so dense,

the seedheads crushed by tires, the wings stuck
wet, they hold the rains, so there's no walkway

dry: so many seeds, and not one will make a
tree, excuse the expression: what of so much

possibility, all impossibility: how about the
one who finds alcohol at eleven, drugs at seventeen

death at thirty-two: how about the little
boy on the street who with puffy-smooth face and

slit eyes reaches up to you for a handshake:
supposing politics swings back like a breeze and

sails tanks through a young crowd: what about the
hopes withered up in screams like crops in

sandy winds: how about the letting out of streams
of blood where rain might have sprinkled into

roadpools: are we to identify with the fortunate
who see the energy of possibility as its necessary

brush with impossibility: who define meaning
only in the blasted landfalls of no meaning:

who can in safety call evil essential to the
differentiations of good: or should we wail

that the lost are lost, that nothing can be right
until they no longer lose themselves, until we've found

charms to call them back: are we to take no
comfort when so much discomfort turns here and

there helplessly for help: is there, in other
words, after the balances are toted up, is there

a streak of light defining the cutting edge as
celebration: (clematis which looks as dead and

drained in winter as baling wire transports in
spring such leaves and plush blooms!) I walked

down the hall to the ward-wing surrounded on
three sides with windows' light and there with

the other diabetics like minnows in the pool-
head of a tidal rising sat my father slumped,

gussied up with straps, in a wheelchair, a catheter leading
to the little fuel tank hung underneath, urine

the color of gasoline, my father like the
others drawn down half-asleep mulling over his

wheels: where, I thought, hope of good is gone
evil becomes the deliverer, and more evil, to get

one through to the clearing where presence, now
pain, enters oblivion: my father roused himself

and took some hope in me but then left me back
alone: at a point in evil, evil changes its

clothes and death with a soft smile crooks its
finger to us: a taking by death leaving the

living bereft: such a mixture! where does a steady
formulation settle down: what integration

of wisdom holds scoured by the bottoms of . . .
bottoms? . . . questioned, I mean, by nibbling

exception and branching direction: every balance
overbalances: judiciousness loses the excitement

of error: realizing that there is no safety
is safety: the other side of anything is worth

nearly as much as the side: the difference
so slight in fact, that one goes out to see if

it is there: I want a curvature like the
arising of a spherical section, a sweep that

doesn't break down from arc into word, image,
definition, story, thesis, but all these

assimilated to an arch of silence, an interrelation
permitting motion in stillness: I want to see

furrows of definition, both the centerings of
furrow and the clumpy outcastings beyond: I do

not want to be caught inside for clarity: I
want clarity to be a smooth long bend

disallowing no complexity in coming clean: why
do I want this, complexity without confusion,

clarity without confinement, time in time, not
time splintered: if you are not gone at a certain

age, your world is: or it is shriveled to a
few people who know what you know: aunts and

uncles with their histories blanked out, the thick
tissue of relationships erased into one of emptiness

or maybe your cousins, too, are gone, and
the world has starved to a single peak,

you and what you know alone, with no one
else in the world to nod recognizing what you

say and recall without explanation: so, have
your choice to leave the world or have it leave

you; either way you choose will bring the same
result, nothingness and the vanishment of

what was: over and over the world rolls in this
wise, so much so that people stricken with these

knowledges think the aspiration to win to be
remembered, to be let hanging, dibbling in the

minds of those continuing: but life is not first
for being remembered but for being lived! how

quaint and sad the lives of those who have lived
but are gone, the vacant sadness of two eternities

pressed together, squeezing them dry to
nondegradable remnants—trash: the meaning,

the tears, loves, sweet handholdings, all
the fears, jealousies, hangings, burnings—

throwaways, obsolescences that plug up
the circulations today, burdening the living

with guilty obligations of memory and service:
to have the curvature, though, one needs the

concisions of the local, contemplations such as
how to slice a banana for breakfast oatmeal,

fourteen thick or thirty-three thin events, the
chunky substance of fourteen encounters or the

flavor availabilities in limp circles: fly the
definite lest it lock you in! have solvent by

should the imperative devise you a vice: see
a spread of possibilities, not an onion plot:

the juggler has twice as many balls as hands
because it's all up in the air: keep it up

in the air, boundingly like ephemera at dusk:
or dawn: I saw in Carolina morning flies

midair like floating stones: the dew, heavy;
the sun, blood red: a road dipping round a

pine grove down a hill to a pond, the spillway
clogged with cattails bent with breezes and with

redwings awilding day: a crippled old farmer
up early with his dog, noon likely to melt tar,

a benchlong of old blacks at the crossroads
gas station, dogfennel high on the woods' edge,

some scraggly roastnear corn used up, tomato
plants sprawled out, become vines: morning,

gentlemen, how you all doing: these bitty
events, near pangs commonplace on this planet

so strangely turned out, we mustn't take on so
but let the music sway, the rhetoric ride, the

garbage heave, for if we allow one solid cast
of grief to flip and filter away into all the

trinklets it might go, we would be averaged
down to a multiple diminishment like acceptance:

but we mean to go on and go on till we unwind
the winding of our longset road, when, we

presume, the nothingness we
step to will mirror treasures we leave, a

strange mirror, everything in our lives having
taken root in love, the sequences having become

right because that is the way they had to run:
but, then, for the trouble of love, we may be

so tired that indifference will join ours to the
hills' indifference and the broad currents of

the deep and the high windings of the sky, and
we may indeed see the ease beyond our

understanding because, till now, always beyond

Anxiety's Prosody

Anxiety clears meat chunks out of the stew, carrots, takes
the skimmer to floats of greasy globules and with
     cheesecloth

filters the broth, looking for the transparent, the
     colorless
essential, the unbeginning and unending of consommé:
     the

open anxiety breezes through thick conceits, surface
      congestions
(it likes metaphors deep-lying, out of sight, their airs
      misting

up into, lighting up consciousness, unidentifiable
      presences),
it distills consonance and assonance, glottal thickets,
      brush

clusters, it thins the rhythms, rushing into longish gaits,
      more
distance in less material time: it hates clots, its stump-
      fires

level fields: patience and calm define borders and
      boundaries,
hedgerows, and sharp whirls: anxiety burns
      instrumentation

matterless, assimilates music into motion, sketches the
      high
suasive turnings, skirts mild natures' tangled, nubby
      clumps.

Eternity's Taciturnity

It's so hard to tell what's missing: you can't
see by what is there: so little is there
that most of the time most everything is missing,

anyhow, intended or not: but all the missing is
easily missed because what is there, little as
it is, fills up the whole sight, blinding away

everything absent: and you can't tell what is
missing because absence leaves no trace: anyway,
I don't say anything about Rome or the architecture

of the Palatine: I say nothing about the Bavarian;
pre- or post-Christian; bureaucracies,
wars, canons, bloody murderers: in

fact, history which gives us the only identity we
have is so terrifying a tale I'd just as soon
wipe it out and keep trying to start over:

if I were to mention anyone, I'd mention old
Enkidu to whom I am unnaturally attracted; probably,
not Gilgamesh, he was so fretful: I almost never

say a word about where I came from: I left there:
please, when you see the little I have, try to
imagine what I've left out: I meant to leave it out.

Boon

I put my head
down low
finally and said

where then do I
belong: your
belonging

is to belong nowhere:
what am I
to be:

your being is to be
about to be:
what am I to

do: show
what doing comes to:
thank

you
for this office,
this use.

Continuity

I've pressed so
far away from
my desire that

if you asked
me what I
want I would,

accepting the harmonious
completion of the
drift, say annihilation,

probably.

FROM **Glare**

I see the eye-level silver shine of
the axe blade the big neighbor carried

at our house at dawn, and I see the
child carried off in arms to the woods,

see the sapling split and the child
passed through and the tree bound

back: as the tree knits, the young
rupture heals: so, great mother of

the muses, let me forget the sharp
edge of the lit blade and childish

unknowing, the trees seeming from
our motion loose in motion, the deep

mysteries playing through the ritual:
let me forget that and so much: let

me who knows so little know less:
alas, though: feeling that is so

fleeting is carved in stone across
the gut: I can't float or heave it

out: it has become a foundation:
whatever is now passes like early

snow on a warm boulder: but the
boulder over and over is revealed,

its grainy size and weight a glare:
rememberers of loveliness, ruddy

glees, how you cling to memory, while
haunted others sweat and wring out

the nights and haste about stricken
through the days: tell me about it:

the truth laid bare is a woman laid
bare: nowhere does the language

provide the truth humped bare, as
with a man: the language travels

close to the bone: sometimes when
you're up against it a few bucks will

get you all the way in: already
top-heavy with bloom, the chrysanthemum

in the yard pot has sprawled broadside
with snow: I hope the pot didn't

crack: that's a nice pot: the
flat-out truth: why am I always

afflicted with things you can't find
like "the poetry section": "pets"

is plain enough, and "young readers"
and "occult": tucked away in a

subdivision of a nook is the poetry
section: sure, *you* find it: but

the salesgirl in the 30%-off section
revealed a slight swell lateral to

the cleavage, but in the 75%-off
section, shaving (or plucking) was

notable along the delta edge: I was
never so pleased in my life: I

bought everything (though I was
actually looking for a book on rhyme

—no such luck): but I love women
so much, even the way you can talk

them into duplicity, I mean their
melting spirituality, like the

rose-warmth of nursing, just moves
me so much, I feel like saying,

please excuse me, but are you sure
it would be all right if I mounted

you: that harsh and greedy move,
with wholesome respect not sufficiently

acknowledged, and the entire enterprise
not sufficiently floated in tenderness?

I don't know about you, but I think
tenderness can be observed even in

the eagerest strokes, so that when
it gets rough it's just as free and

easy as playing with the wind: I
bought a pair of shoes for ice: a

gritty or cusp-crested sole suctions
the slick: the man behind me, a

young fellow with his wife, had an
extra $2 coupon he gave me: can

you imagine: I wished him and her a
Happy Thanksgiving, I was that

thankful: this strip is so narrow:
a rhythm cannot unwind across it:

it cracks my shoulder blades with
pressing confinement: the next time

I take up prosody, I'm not going to
take up this

———

money, enhancing the fluency of negotiation,
has no substance of its own: it

is just medium, action, the flow by
which substances are exchanged,

the system by which desire seeks the
most nearly total and "spiritual"

negotiation between wish and wished-for:
money transmits, transforms, "stands

for," catalyzes—and yet is nothing
in itself, an airy agreement between

desirers, valueless when no longer
valued, iconic and flat when no longer

current: language operates the same
way: it holds its consistences,

designations, forms, economies in
currencies, in motions: let fall

from negotiation, language disappears
as languages have often done, without

any lasting effect to the material
world—the language had added

nothing to and taken nothing from the
economy whose exchanges it had

sustained: write a poem about boulders
or feathers and the net weight of the

world is unchanged: riffle a manuscript
of poems into the sea—one, let's

say, containing much wisdom of human
experience—and the manuscript is

lost, the ink slides free, returning
as much weight to the world as it had

taken from it:

———

how wonderful to be able to write:
it's something you can't do, like

playing the piano, without thinking:
it's not important thinking, but the

strip has to wind, the right keys
have to be hit, you have to look to

see if you're spelling the words
right: maybe it's not the thinking

but the concentration, which means
the attention is directed outside

and focused away from the self, away
from obsessive self-monitorings:

these self-monitorings create problems
where there are none: they fill

inanition with misery, when if you
can look about and do things,

inanition goes away and so does the
misery: but I, I have a long history

of misery: I've suffered enough, I
should know how: it has come off and

on often enough, I should expect it:
but sometimes it has gone away for

years and then the return is difficult:
I have to (you, one has to) learn all

over again how to cope: one thing
one learns, I suppose, is that there

is little poetic value in writing
about misery: so many other things

to most people are more interesting:
almost anything is: a few of those

little rug moths fly up this time of
year and light on the walls: I get

some of them with a fly swatter, but
I don't know that that helps cure the

moth problem: when do they mate:
when do they lay eggs: how do they

know what to do: they probably do
it without thinking: the way I

write: I write to write: it's
not that I think that's the way to

write: it's that this way of writing
occupies me: it's a way of existing

that is more comfortable than not
writing: most writers, of course,

take pains, as I'm sure they should,
to write and to write well: I don't

mean to say this is good in spite of
my nonchalance, and I don't mean to

demean the reader (what?) by asking
him to spend his time on time merely

spent: since I started this, 15
fairly pleasant minutes have passed:

my gratitude for that is, like,
boundless: I am encouraged to think

that maybe I can get through the
whole weekend by writing when I need

to: when I can't find anything
(better?) to do: believe me, I wd

not do this if I were better connected,
if I were better engaged: walking

is good, but the knee joint in my
deveined leg hurts (the whole leg

swells in the heat): swimming is
nice, but I gave up my membership

when I got sick: reading is sometimes
possible: when I can read nothing

else, sometimes I can read what I
have written (that's usually innocent

and nonviolent enough): I've said
before that I write so I'll have

something to read, and that does
double the pleasure and the time the

pleasure takes: I am basically in
perfect health: but right now I

have things in the future to do that
seem like a threat: these things

are not threats but exciting
opportunities: I have just twisted

them around to where I'm *afraid* I
can't do them, and that is threatening:

as a matter of record, usually when
I do such things (such as poetry

readings or dinners with presidents
(of colleges or universities) I do

them well enough to make people
kind: what could be less threatening

than kindness: it is much less
threatening, say, than love, which

is so invasive and deeply involving:

———

sometimes I get the feeling I've never
lived here at all, and 31 years seem

no more than nothing: I have to stop
and think, oh, yeah, there was the

kid, so much anguish over his allergy,
and there was the year we moved to

another house, and oh, yes, I remember
the lilies we planted near that

siberian elm, and there was the year
they made me a professor, and the

year, right in the middle of a long
poem, when I got blood poisoning from

an ingrown toenail not operated on
right: but a wave slices through,

canceling everything, and the space
with nothing to fill it shrinks and

time collapses, so that nothing happened,
and I didn't exist, and existence

itself seems like a wayward temporizing,
an illusion nonexistence sometimes

stumbles into: keep your mind open,
something might crawl in: which

reminds me of my greatest saying:
old poets never die, they just scrawl

away: and then I think of my friends
who may have longed for me, and I say

oh, I'll be here the next time
around: alas, the next time will

not come next: so what am I to say
to friends who know I'm not here and

won't be back: I'm sorry I missed
you guys: but even with the little

I know I loved you a lot, a lot more
than I said: our mountains here are

so old they're hills: they've been
around around 300 million years but

indifference in all that time broke
itself only to wear them out: my

indifference is just like theirs: it
wipes itself clear: surely, I will have

another chance: surely, nothing is
let go till trouble free: when

I come back I'm going to be there
every time: and then the wave that

comes to blank me out will be set
edgy and jiggling with my recalcitrance

and my consciousness will take on weight

Shot Glass

I'll never forget the day this beautiful woman
right out in the office said I was "sneaky":

I didn't know I was sneaky: I didn't feel
sneaky: but there are mechanisms below our

mechanisms, so I assume the lady was right:
living with that has not helped my progress

in the world, if there is any such thing,
progress, I mean: also it has hurt my image

of myself: I have used up so much fellow-
feeling on the general—all of which I have

forgotten specifically about, as have the
fellows—no offices, no clear images or

demonstrations—I don't understand why that
one remark holds its place ungivingly in me:

and now to talk about it, admit to the world
(my reading public, as it happens) that I am

scarred by an old, old wound about to heal and
about to bleed: this may do confessional good

but I will no longer appear perfect to others:
conceivably, that could be a good thing:

others may be scarred, too, but who wants to
be like them: one should: perhaps I really

do, because lonely splendor is devastatingly
shiny but basically hard and cold, marble

walls and glistening floors: one comfort,
which I am reluctant to relish, is that the

lady is now dead—surely, I am sorry about that,
she was a person of intelligence and

discernment, which is one reason she hurt me
so bad—well, but I mean, she won't hurt

anybody else: she probably did enough good
in her life that the Lord will forgive her:

I am trying to forgive her myself: after all
she left me some room for improvement and

a sense of what to work on. . . .

Birthday Poem to My Wife

Have you considered how inconsequential we all
are: I mean, in the long term: but

anything getting closer to now—deaths, births,
marriages, murders—grows the consequence

till if you kissed me that would be a matter
of great consequence: large spaces also include

us into anonymity, but you beside me, as the
proximity heightens, declares myself, and you, to

the stars: not a galaxy refuses its part in
spelling our names: thus you understand if you

go out in the back yard or downtown to the
grocery store—or take a plane to Paris—

time pours in around me and space
devours me and like inconsequence I'm little and lost.

A Few Acres of Shiny Water

I guess anything gets old: being rich, yep,
pretty soon it's old—occasional pleasant

spurts of realization, then—celebrity, a big
ox in your way wherever you turn, that gets

old: having nothing to do gets old in a hurry,
going from having something to do to not being

able to find anything to do, I'll say: being
in love, oh, dear, even that, about the third

month, gets old as hell, all those re-arisings:
on the bestseller list—great the first week,

also the second week; then it's every week,
expected, tedious, getting old: market up,

wow, up again, oh, boy, still up, up and up,
I see, okay, really: you are finally thought

to be as good a poet as you thought—so; so
what, what is a poet: even getting old gets

old, the novelty aches and pains, surprising
and scary at first, they don't wear off but

the novelty does: finding, and trying to
find, something new gets old: find a new

risk to take, a new cliff to sail off from,
pretty soon it's a drag to get all the way to

Nepal or a Filipino trench: telling about
getting old and everything getting old gets

old, I'll tell you, it sure does. . . .

In View of the Fact

The people of my time are passing away: my
wife is baking for a funeral, a 60-year-old who

died suddenly, when the phone rings, and it's
Ruth we care so much about in intensive care:

it was once weddings that came so thick and
fast, and then, first babies, such a hullabaloo:

now, it's this that and the other and somebody
else gone or on the brink: well, we never

thought we would live forever (although we did)
and now it looks like we won't: some of us

are losing a leg to diabetes, some don't know
what they went downstairs for, some know that

a hired watchful person is around, some like
to touch the cane tip into something steady,

so nice: we have already lost so many,
brushed the loss of ourselves ourselves: our

address books for so long a slow scramble now
are palimpsests, scribbles and scratches: our

index cards for Christmases, birthdays,
Halloweens drop clean away into sympathies:

at the same time we are getting used to so
many leaving, we are hanging on with a grip

to the ones left: we are not giving up on the
congestive heart failure or brain tumors, on

the nice old men left in empty houses or on
the widows who decide to travel a lot: we

think the sun may shine someday when we'll
drink wine together and think of what used to

be: until we die we will remember every
single thing, recall every word, love every

loss: then we will, as we must, leave it to
others to love, love that can grow brighter

and deeper till the very end, gaining strength
and getting more precious all the way. . . .

Speaking

There will be rains I'll need
no shelter from; cold winds
no walls need broach the chill of for me:

when fire splits seams
out of the ground, I won't
need the warmth at all: love, even,

when you who have given
your days to me, when you
come close, I won't sense

that last approach: not
knowing how to speak,
I'll say nothing.

Frumpy Cronies

Is it possible my wife had heard in the next
room on TV someone mention cluster earrings

a few minutes before she said her headaches—
these fugitive little seizures about the

brain—come in clusters: I said, how do you
mean clusters, and she said, you have them for

a few days, and then they go away: I said I
would like to come in clusters, such an awful

joke we both tried to laugh: my favorite word
in that area is one my student Lisa Steinman

used to use in her poems—clumps: that is
so cool a word: I wish I could remember some

of her lines, though I have not forgotten the
one about a messenger pigeon that got in some

kind of accident but was coming up the lane
walking with a bandaged leg anyhow, the message

bound to the other leg: Lisa teaches
at Reed, now: a little bitty woman, she always

had three big sacks hanging off her various
parts, books in some, supplies, I think, in

others for the 20-or-so member commune she was
forever taking part of cooking for: what

a lovely, lovely poet she was and looking like
a touch of a clump herself: oh, my memories:

they are so small and so sweet: aphids, you
know, cluster: they get out toward the tips

where the greens are tender: and galloping
dominoes form little crusts, dark crusts, where

they suckle: and water beetles whirling on
branch water will clump up into

swirls: galaxies, for heaven's sake, they,
too, vaguely attract each other: not to make

too much of it, clumping sounds like something
suddenly falling together, I like that.

22 March '98

Shuffled Marbles

Old men don't care who they talk to, I
don't know if you've ever noticed: they'll

say to a stranger stepped into the elevator,
so, where are you going today, or

absorbed in a monologue, they'll turn
suddenly to you as if you'd been there all the

time: these meaningless contorts from the irrelevant
baffle people, or else they just keep their

chins straight ahead as if they'd never been
called on: I want to say, what's it

to you, you old fiddler twanger: old myself
I look into the panel mirror and wonder if

I just spoke to myself: by that time the
elevator has stopped somewhere: I get off.

23 March '98

Don't Rush on My Account

The crows around here are getting to be as big
as eagles: maybe it's the morning blahs but

when they swoosh in behind the branches they
look like marauders: l can feel them picking

fish out of the creeks of my head: trios of
caws mingle and scrawl: that lady down the

street feeds them slices of white bread in
winter: winters don't lean them up: they

know the difference between bread and snow, and
many a January morning they've arrived before

the late day and are ruffling in the trees: oh,
yes, I wouldn't be surprised, they are evolving

and I can't imagine into what, something bigger:
their prominent peckers which they put to such

expert use, I hope they don't get any bigger:
I also fear the feet: nobody wants bigger

crowsfeet: those pincer claws could grasp your
scalp, and heads could drop their peckers over

and swallow your eyeballs: but a scattering
of killed squirrels on the winter roads, a

warm spell here and there getting the flea-bitten
little rascals out, that keeps a running

streak, if half-starved, of protein going, then
a few bundles of green-bud on bushes (and, of

course, the white slices) and you have a pretty
good chance of setting up the circumstances

for dramatic shifts to cruel cousins of the
sky, a chancy day. . . .

29/30 March '98

Run Ragged

I said I don't want to be older, but it's be older
and older or nothing, right: and day by day

it's been older every day since the beginning:
still, there was a bracket of young years

within which one could say, these are not the
older years or the baby years: there are, as

Shakespeare said, groups of time, the
transitions from one group to another usually

unalarming: people who have nothing to say
should say nothing: they should drum syllables

or squeeze verbs (or nouns) or cast them like
die, craps, creeps: for example, I don't

feel at home in this universe and it may be
the only one: that is so pathetic: I think

that is so heartrending with content:
how can the place you come from not be your

home: is the only way to make a phrase
interesting to make it sound like it's not a

phrase: or it could be two phrases or go two
different ways when you are really going nowhere

well, the human race needs a better track,
the track itself worn or grown over.

31 March '98

———

When the bubbles of nothingness rise
out of nothing—
a fine and brittle crust like
blown glass, cooled motion, forms
and in the rough spots
chinks of someday
we have our lives
build wars, consider
prophets, and
carefully seek to know
what robe or crown to wear

1 April '98

BIOGRAPHICAL NOTE

NOTE ON THE TEXTS

INDEX OF TITLES AND FIRST LINES

BIOGRAPHICAL NOTE

Archie Randolph Ammons was born on February 18, 1926, in Whiteville, North Carolina, the youngest of his parents' three surviving children. His father worked as a tobacco farmer. After graduating high school Ammons worked at the naval shipyard in Wilmington, North Carolina; as a member of the U.S. Naval Reserve during World War II, he served on board a destroyer escort in the South Pacific. After the war he studied biology at Wake Forest College, receiving his degree in 1949; in the 1950s, he took graduate courses in English at the University of California at Berkeley. He married Phyllis Plumbo in 1949. Ammons spent a year as the principal of an elementary school on the Outer Banks of North Carolina, and later worked for several years as a sales executive for a glass company in southern New Jersey. *Ommateum*, his first collection of poetry, was published at his own expense in 1955. In 1964 he joined the faculty of the English Department at Cornell University, where he would teach for more than three decades. A popular teacher and prolific poet, Ammons published more than 20 volumes of poetry, as well as the prose collection *Set in Motion* (1996). He received numerous awards, including a MacArthur Fellowship, a Guggenheim Fellowship, the Lannon Poetry Prize, a

Fellowship from the American Academy and Institute of Arts and Letters, a Bollingen Prize (1975) for *Sphere: The Form of a Motion*, and National Book Awards for *Collected Poems 1951–1971* in 1973, and for *Garbage* in 1993. He died of cancer on February 25, 2001.

NOTE ON THE TEXTS

In the present volume, the poems from "So I Said I Am Ezra" to "Poetics" and from "Dominion" to "The City Lights" are taken from *Collected Poems 1951–1971* (New York: Norton, 1972), reprinted by permission. The other poems printed here are taken from the following sources:

Excerpt from *Tape for the Turn of the Year*: *Tape for the Turn of the Year* (Ithaca, N.Y.: Cornell University Press, 1965), reprinted by permission, of W. W. Norton & Co.

For Harold Bloom; excerpt from *Sphere*: *Sphere: The Form of a Motion* (New York: Norton, 1974), reprinted by permission.

Ballad: *Diversifications* (New York: Norton, 1975), reprinted by permission.

One Must Recall as One Mourns the Dead; The Perfect Journey Is; You Can't Imitate; Some Nights I Go Out to Piss: *The Snow Poems* (New York: Norton, 1977), reprinted by permission.

In Memoriam Mae Noblitt; Easter Morning; Sunday at McDonald's; Poverty: *A Coast of Trees* (New York: Norton, 1981), reprinted by permission.

Immoderation; The Role of Society in the Artist; Shit List; or, Omnium-gatherum of Diversity into Unity; Immortality: *Worldly Hopes* (New York: Norton, 1982), reprinted by permission.

The Fairly High Assimilation Rag; I Could Not Be Here At All: *Lake Effect Country* (New York: Norton, 1983), reprinted by permission.

Autonomy: *Sumerian Vistas* (New York: Norton, 1987), reprinted by permission.

Their Sex Life; For Louise and Tom Gossett: *The Really Short Poems of A.R. Ammons* (New York: Norton, 1990), reprinted by permission.

INDEX OF TITLES
AND FIRST LINES

AMERICAN POETS PROJECT